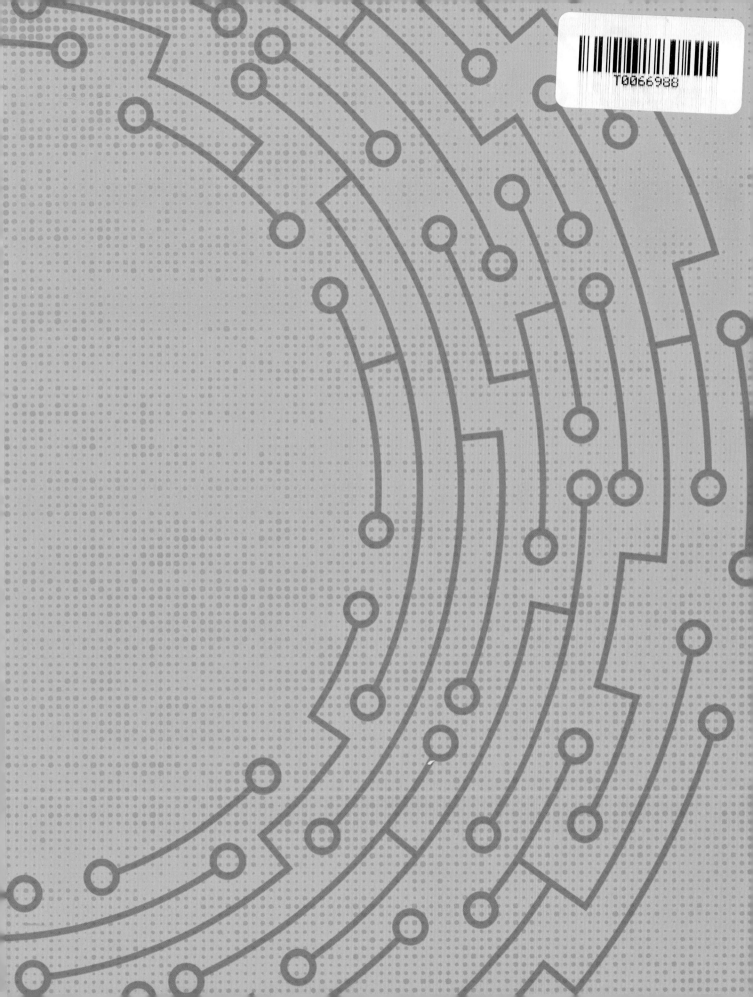

CREATE THE CODE

SOUND AND VIDEO

Max Wainewright

First published in Great Britain in 2020
by Wayland

Text copyright © ICT Apps, 2020
Art and design copyright © Hodder and
Stoughton, 2020

Editor: Elise Short
Designer: Matt Lilly
Cover design: Peter Scoulding
Illustrations: John Haslam

Every attempt has been made
to clear copyright.

Should there be any inadvertent
omission, please apply to the publisher
for rectification.

ISBN: 978-1-4380-8937-9

All inquiries should be addressed to:
Peterson's Publishing, LLC
4380 S. Syracuse Street, Suite 200
Denver, CO 80237-2624
www.petersonsbooks.com

B.E.S.

Printed and bound in China

MIX
Paper from
responsible sources
FSC® C104740
www.fsc.org

Picture credits:
iStock: AtomStudios 5cl; Maica 4c;
PeopleImages 5cr; RollingEarth 21b.
Shutterstock:Guiliano DelMoretto 5t;
nikkytok 7b.

We recommend that children are supervised at all times when using the Internet. Some of the projects in this series use a computer webcam or microphone. Please make sure children are made aware that they should only allow a computer to access the webcam or microphone on specific websites that a trusted adult has told them to use. We do not recommend children use websites or microphones on any websites other than those mentioned in this book.

The website addresses (URLs) included in this book were valid at the time of going to press. However, it is possible that contents or addresses may have changed since the publication of this book. No responsibility for any such changes can be accepted by either the author or the Publisher.

Scratch is developed by the Lifelong Kindergarten Group at the MIT Media Lab. See http://scratch.mit.edu. Images and illustrations from Scratch included in this book have been developed by the Lifelong Kindergarten Group at the MIT Media Lab (see http://scratch.mit.edu) and made available under the Creative Commons Attribution-ShareAlike 2.0 licence (https://creativecommons.org/licenses/by-sa/2.0/deed.en). The third party trademarks used in this book are the property of their respective owners, including the Scratch name and logo. The owners of these trademarks have not endorsed, authorised or sponsored this book.

Contents

For help with any of the projects go to: www.maxw.com

Sound and Video

Computers can be used to record and play back real sounds. They can also create or "synthesize" new sounds. In this book you'll learn how to use code to play and change both sorts of sounds, and to code your own music. You will also find out how to use code to capture video, how to play it back with special effects, and how to add videos from sharing sites to an HTML page.

Digitizing Sound

For a computer to record a sound, it needs to convert what the microphone picks up from a sound wave into data (information understood by a computer). You can then use code to play the sound back. See page 8 to find out more about digitizing sound.

Synthesizing Sound

Computers can also synthesize (produce electronically) sounds that haven't been recorded. This method makes it easy for code to change the pitch of a sound, which is how high or how low the sound is. Changing the pitch using code is how music keyboards work. Learn how to code a music keyboard on page 10.

MIDI

Synthesized sounds have been around since the early 20th century. In 1983, a way of connecting different electronic instruments together called MIDI was developed. This stands for Musical Instrument Digital Interface. MIDI typically allows 128 different synthesized instruments to be played on a keyboard including a piano, xylophone, various organs, guitars and violins, trombones, and many more. You can experiment with some of these in the projects on pages 10-15.

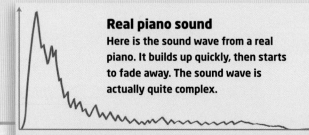

Real piano sound
Here is the sound wave from a real piano. It builds up quickly, then starts to fade away. The sound wave is actually quite complex.

Digitized piano sound
Early MIDI digitized sound waves broke the sound into four sections and simplified the wave. The steps were called: 1 Attack, 2 Decay, 3 Sustain, and 4 Release.

Video

A video or movie consists of a series of still images, shown one after another. Before digital video was around, moving pictures were stored on film. The first film systems used 16 frames (pictures) per second and were filmed in black and white. These were silent movies with no sound. Over the years film technology developed to include sound and color.

In the 1980s, the first video cameras for home use were introduced. They stored video on videotapes (right). By the early 1990s, digital video cameras went on sale. Instead of storing video on videotapes, they were stored as data on digital disks or memory cards.

Now digital cameras have become very small, light, and cheap. Every year their performance improves. They can be integrated into phones, tablets, computers, cars, and even pens!

Here's a videotape from the 1980s.

Coding Video

You'll learn how to display video from a web cam.

Using simple code, you'll learn how to add color filters to the image.

You'll be using Scratch blocks to change the color of the video image.

```
when  clicked
turn video  on ▼
set video transparency to  50
```

We will find out how to add a video player to a web page using HTML code.

documents/video.html

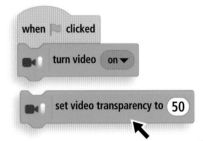

We will also learn to control the video using JavaScript.

```
<video>
    <source src="slide.mp4>
</video>
```

```
function playVideo(){
    vp.play();
{
```

5

Drums

Let's create an electronic drum kit.

To play the drums, you'll either click on each drum or press keys on the computer keyboard. The drum sounds are real recorded drum sounds built into Scratch.

STEP 1: Start Scratch

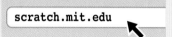

Open your web browser and type in **scratch.mit.edu**

Press the **enter** key.

Click **Create** to get started.

STEP 2: No cats

Click the blue x to delete the cat sprite.

STEP 3: Add a sprite

Click the **Choose a Sprite** button.

Select the **Music** group.

Drum Kit

Scroll through and click on **Drum Kit**.

STEP 4: Code the drum

Drag in these blocks to the **Scripts** area.

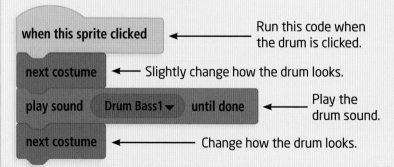

Run this code when the drum is clicked.

Slightly change how the drum looks.

Play the drum sound.

Change how the drum looks.

Now try clicking the drum to test your code.

STEP 5: Key press

Add more code to play the drum when the 1 key is pressed.

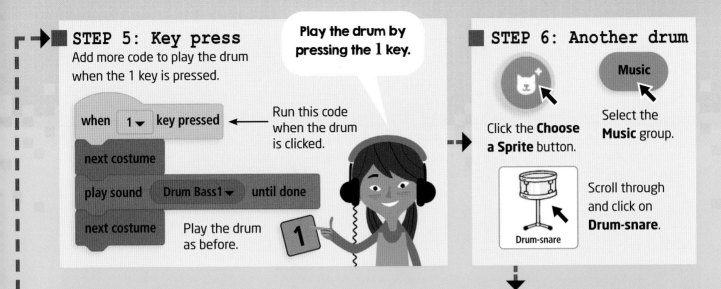

when [1 ▾] key pressed ← Run this code when the drum is clicked.

next costume

play sound [Drum Bass1 ▾] until done

next costume → Play the drum as before.

Play the drum by pressing the 1 key.

STEP 6: Another drum

Click the **Choose a Sprite** button.

Select the **Music** group.

Scroll through and click on **Drum-snare**.

Drum-snare

STEP 7: Add code

Drag in these blocks to the **Scripts** area.

Add this code so it plays when the 2 key is pressed:

when this sprite clicked ← Run this code when the drum is clicked.

next costume ← Change how the drum looks.

play sound [tap snare ▾] until done ← Play the snare sound.

next costume ← Change how the drum looks.

Now try clicking the new snare drum to test your code.

when [2 ▾] key pressed

next costume

play sound [tap snare ▾] until done

next costume

Try pressing the 2 key.

STEP 8: More drums, more code

Repeat steps 7 and 8 to add more drums.

Electronic drum kits

Electronic drum kits are a more portable alternative to a real set of drums. In the example here, drum sticks are used to hit a set of pads. The pads are actually switches, which are used to trigger the drum sounds. Smaller drum machines just use simple buttons for each drum.

The sounds are either digitally synthesized or use a digital recording of a real drum sound. Most drum machines have features to allow drummers to record a drum pattern and play it back. The pattern can then be sped up or slowed down. The drum machine can be plugged into an amplifier to make it louder.

Recording Sound

Now let's use the microphone in your computer and Scratch to record some real sounds.

We'll use code to play back the sound over and over in a loop. By using other short pieces of code, we will try changing the volume and the speed of the sound.

Converting an analog sound

 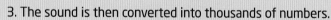

1. An analog sound wave keeps changing.

2. When it is digitized the wave is measured up to 44,000 times per second.

3. The sound is then converted into thousands of numbers.

```
33 40 48 61 74 82 83 77 65
46 32 19 -19 -22 -33 -76
-82 -94 -88 -76 -43 -33
-25 3 45 48 61 74 82 83 77
65 46 32 19 -19 -22 -33
-76 -82 -94 -88 -76 -43
-33 -25 3 76 -82 -94 -88
-76 -43 -33 -25 3 45 48 6
77 65 46 32 19 77 65 46 32
19 48 61 74 82 55 67 -5 -7
```

4. These numbers are turned into binary code (1s and 0s) and stored in a file.

```
11111111110101101
011010010010010010
010101010100110101
011101011111101101
101001001010010010
101010110101010101
010010010010101011
110101110111011101
111010010101010001
```

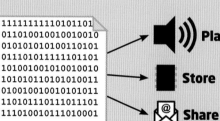

Play

Store

Share

The sound can then be played, stored, or shared.

We can record sounds straight into Scratch, then use code to play them.

STEP 1: Start Scratch

`scratch.mit.edu`

Start Scratch and click **Create**.

STEP 2: Choose Sounds

Sounds

Choose the **Sounds** tab.

STEP 3: Choose Record

Let your mouse hover over the **Choose a Sound** button.

Record

Click **Record**.

You need a microphone for your computer for this project. There may already be one built into it. If not, you need to plug one in. Make sure it is selected and turned up by checking the settings program in your computer.

STEP 4: Record your sound

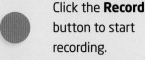

Click the **Record** button to start recording.

Stop recording

Click **Stop recording** when you are finished.

Save

Click **Save**.

Your sound wave will show up here.

Record Sound

Record

STEP 5: Start coding

Code

Click the **Code** tab, then drag these blocks to the **Scripts** area.

when ⚑ clicked ← Run this code when the green flag is clicked.

clear sound effects ← This resets the sound back to normal.

forever ← Keep repeating the following line of code.

play sound recording1 ▼ until done ← Play back the sound you just recorded.

⚑ Click the green flag to run the code. You should hear your sound played back repeatedly.

STEP 6: Change volume and speed

Add these four separate pieces of code:

when up arrow ▼ key pressed
change volume by 10
← When **up** is pressed, make the sound louder.

when down arrow ▼ key pressed
change volume by -10
← When **down** is pressed, make the sound quieter (-10 turns the volume down).

when left arrow ▼ key pressed
change pitch ▼ effect by -10
← When **left** is pressed, make the sound slower and lower in pitch.

when right arrow ▼ key pressed
change pitch ▼ effect by 10
← When **right** is pressed, make the sound faster and higher in pitch.

⚑ Click the green flag to run the code. You should hear your sound played back repeatedly.

⬆️ ⬇️ ⬅️ ➡️

EXPERIMENT

Change the values in step 6 from 10 and -10 to 5 and -5. What happens? Try 20 and -20.

Repeat steps 3 and 4 to record another sound. Change the **play sound** drop down to **recording2** or the name of your new sound.

Music Keyboard

So far we have used recorded or digitized sounds. In this project, we will start to code synthesized sounds.

This will allow us to change the pitch easily and create a music keyboard. By changing the instrument, we will be able to play various electronic instruments.

STEP 1: Start Scratch

`scratch.mit.edu`

Start Scratch and click **Create**.

STEP 2: Music extension

Add the Music extension.

Click **Add Extension**.

Music

Click **Music**.

> **The Music Extension adds some extra code blocks to create and control synthesized sounds.**

STEP 3: No cats

Sprite1

Click the blue x to delete the cat sprite.

STEP 4: Add some code

Drag in these blocks to the **Scripts** area.

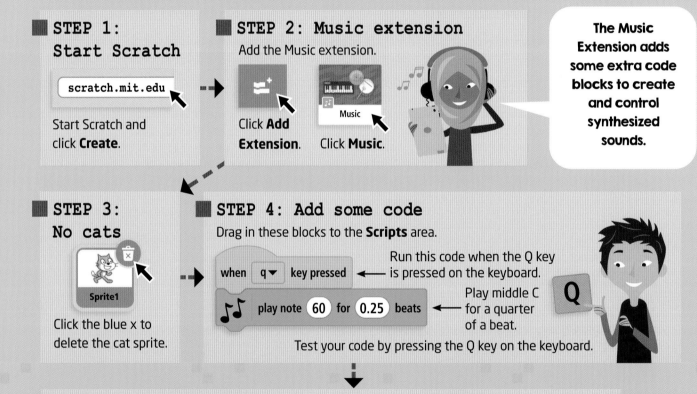

when `q ▼` key pressed ◄— Run this code when the Q key is pressed on the keyboard.

play note `60` for `0.25` beats ◄— Play middle C for a quarter of a beat.

Test your code by pressing the Q key on the keyboard.

STEP 5: Another note

Add these code blocks for the next note.

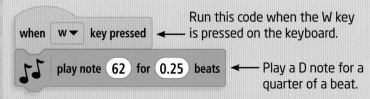

when `w ▼` key pressed ◄— Run this code when the W key is pressed on the keyboard.

play note `62` for `0.25` beats ◄— Play a D note for a quarter of a beat.

Test your code by pressing the W key on the keyboard.

Coding musical notes

Click the note box in the **play note code** block. You can type in a number. The higher the number, the higher the note. To make things easier, a mini piano keyboard will also drop down for you to pick a note to play.

This value tells Scratch how long to play the note. 0.25 means a quarter of a beat. Try changing this value to play longer or shorter notes.

In Scratch, each number corresponds to a semi tone—one key on the piano. There are 12 semitones in an octave (C, C#, D, D#, E, F, F#, G, G#, A, A#, B).

Scratch uses the note value to work out the frequency of the sound to make.

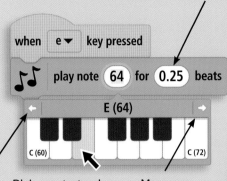

Move down an **octave** lower.

Pick a note to play.

Move an **octave** higher.

Now we need to code more keys to complete the octave.

STEP 6: An octave

Add these code blocks for the next note.

Play each of the keys **Q**, **W**, **E**, **R**, **T**, **Y**, **U**, and **I** to test your code.

STEP 7: Different instruments

Use these code blocks to set a new instrument.

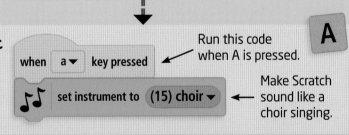

Run this code when A is pressed.

Make Scratch sound like a choir singing.

Press A, then play a tune on the other keys!

EXPERIMENT

Change the instrument in step 7. Can you add code so that different keys select different instruments?

Add more code to play C# when the 2 key is pressed, and D# when 3 is pressed. Can you add all the other black notes in the octave?

Try changing all your code to make it play a whole octave lower. (Remember there are 12 semitones in an octave.)

Use the number keys at the top of the keyboard to add the sharp and flat notes. Start by adding code to play note C# (61) when the number 2 key is played.

Simple Music Sequencer

This project shows you how to set up a number of different musical sequences.

Some sequences will play drums, bass sounds, or simple melodies. Pressing keys allows you to combine these sequences together.

STEP 1: Start Scratch

scratch.mit.edu

Open Scratch and click **Create**.

STEP 2: Music extension

Add the Music extension.

Click **Add Extension**.

Click **Music**.

STEP 3: No cats

Sprite1

Click the blue x to delete the cat sprite.

STEP 4: Add some drums

Drag in these blocks to the **Scripts** area.

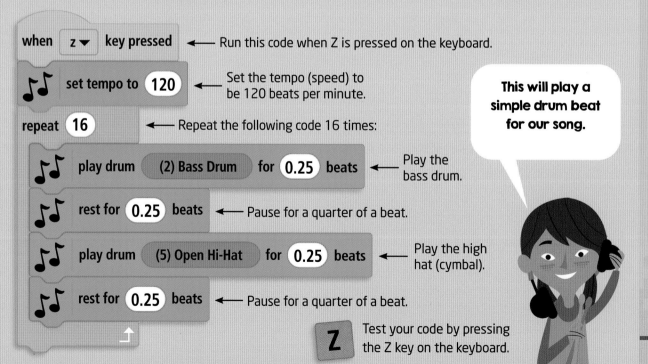

when z ▼ key pressed ← Run this code when Z is pressed on the keyboard.

set tempo to 120 ← Set the tempo (speed) to be 120 beats per minute.

repeat 16 ← Repeat the following code 16 times:

play drum (2) Bass Drum for 0.25 beats ← Play the bass drum.

rest for 0.25 beats ← Pause for a quarter of a beat.

play drum (5) Open Hi-Hat for 0.25 beats ← Play the high hat (cymbal).

rest for 0.25 beats ← Pause for a quarter of a beat.

This will play a simple drum beat for our song.

Z — Test your code by pressing the Z key on the keyboard.

STEP 5: Add some bass

Add these code blocks to create a low bass pattern for the song.

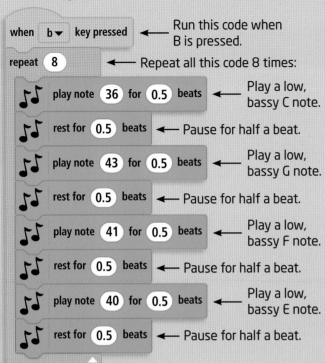

when `b ▾` key pressed ← Run this code when B is pressed.

repeat `8` ← Repeat all this code 8 times:

play note `36` for `0.5` beats ← Play a low, bassy C note.

rest for `0.5` beats ← Pause for half a beat.

play note `43` for `0.5` beats ← Play a low, bassy G note.

rest for `0.5` beats ← Pause for half a beat.

play note `41` for `0.5` beats ← Play a low, bassy F note.

rest for `0.5` beats ← Pause for half a beat.

play note `40` for `0.5` beats ← Play a low, bassy E note.

rest for `0.5` beats ← Pause for half a beat.

B Try your code by pressing B on the keyboard. While it's playing, press the Z key to hear the drums too.

EXPERIMENT

Add a **set instrument** code block and try something other than the piano. Try Synth Lead or Vibraphone.

Try changing the tempo in box 4.

Edit the melodies and try adding some more of your own.

Add some other sprites to your project. Can you make them move or dance as the music plays?

Look back at the keyboard code from page 10. Can you combine this sequencer with the keyboard code so you can play your own melodies over the top of the sequencer sounds?

STEP 6: Add melodies

Drag some code blocks in to create a sequence of notes—a melody.

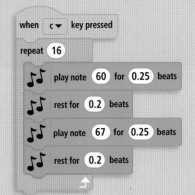

when `c ▾` key pressed

repeat `16`

play note `60` for `0.25` beats

rest for `0.2` beats

play note `67` for `0.25` beats

rest for `0.2` beats

C Test this code by pressing C. Try pressing Z and B to mix the sounds together.

Add another faster and higher melody to your song.

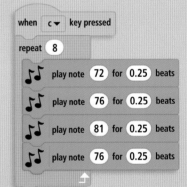

when `c ▾` key pressed

repeat `8`

play note `72` for `0.25` beats

play note `76` for `0.25` beats

play note `81` for `0.25` beats

play note `76` for `0.25` beats

X Try this code by pressing X. Now press Z and B and C at different times to mix the song together.

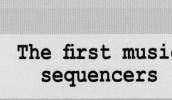

The first music sequencers

Music boxes were the first music sequencers. A series of bumps on a small metal cylinder represent the notes to be played. As the handle is turned, the bumps hit against tiny chimes causing each note to be played in the correct sequence. During the 1950s, programmers started coding computer sequencers, but it wasn't until the 1980s that they became popular in recording studios.

Sound Effects

Now for some sound effects.

By quickly changing the pitch of the sound being played, we can make our own sound effects. To change the pitch, we'll use something called a variable to store the value of the note being played. A change code block will then be used to make the pitch go up or down.

STEP 1: Start Scratch

scratch.mit.edu

Start Scratch and click **Create**.

STEP 2: Music extension

Add the Music extension.

 Click **Add Extension**.

 Click **Music**.

Music

STEP 3: Add a variable

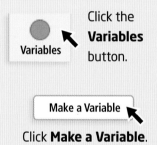 Click the **Variables** button.

Variables

Make a Variable

Click **Make a Variable**.

New Variable

New variable name:

tone

◉ For all sprites   ○

Cancel   OK

Type in **tone** then click **OK**.

The tone variable will store the pitch of the sound that is played.

STEP 4: Add code

Drag in these blocks to the **Scripts** area to make the sound effect play.

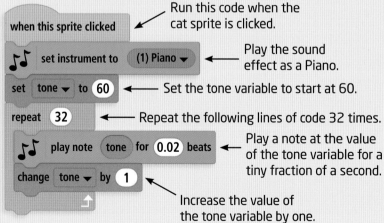

Run this code when the cat sprite is clicked.

Play the sound effect as a Piano.

Set the tone variable to start at 60.

Repeat the following lines of code 32 times.

Play a note at the value of the tone variable for a tiny fraction of a second.

Increase the value of the tone variable by one.

Click the cat to play the sound effect and test the code.

STEP 5: Add a sprite

 Click the choose **new sprite** button.

Wizard Hat

Scroll down and click on **Wizard Hat**.

STEP 6: Add code

Drag in these blocks to the **Scripts** area to make the sound effect play.

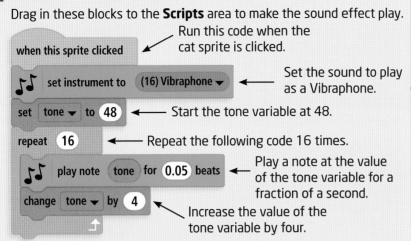

when this sprite clicked — Run this code when the cat sprite is clicked.

set instrument to (16) Vibraphone ▾ — Set the sound to play as a Vibraphone.

set tone ▾ to 48 — Start the tone variable at 48.

repeat 16 — Repeat the following code 16 times.

play note tone for 0.05 beats — Play a note at the value of the tone variable for a fraction of a second.

change tone ▾ by 4 — Increase the value of the tone variable by four.

Click the hat to test the code and play the sound effect.

STEP 7: Add another sprite

Click the choose **new sprite** button.

Rocketship

Scroll down and click on **Rocketship**.

EXPERIMENT

Try changing the number of times each of the **repeat loops** run. What happens?

Experiment with different musical instrument settings.

Alter the amount the tone variable is changed in some of the loops. Try using negative and positive numbers.

Add another sprite to the project. Add some more code and create your own sound effect. How much will you change the tone variable by? Try using more than one loop and making the sound go up and down.

STEP 8: Code the rocket

Add this code to make a sound effect for the rocket.

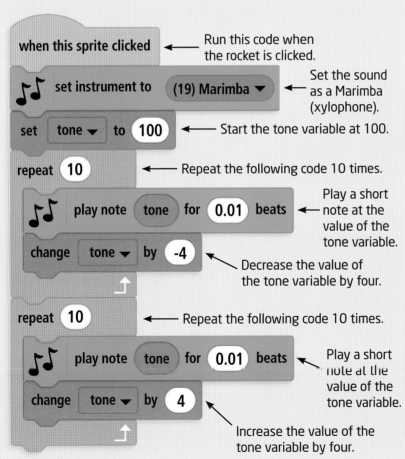

when this sprite clicked — Run this code when the rocket is clicked.

set instrument to (19) Marimba ▾ — Set the sound as a Marimba (xylophone).

set tone ▾ to 100 — Start the tone variable at 100.

repeat 10 — Repeat the following code 10 times.

play note tone for 0.01 beats — Play a short note at the value of the tone variable.

change tone ▾ by -4 — Decrease the value of the tone variable by four.

repeat 10 — Repeat the following code 10 times.

play note tone for 0.01 beats — Play a short note at the value of the tone variable.

change tone ▾ by 4 — Increase the value of the tone variable by four.

Some computers play very short sounds slightly differently. If you don't hear anything, try using a different instrument number.

Text-based Coding

In the next few projects we will look at using more advanced coding techniques. You will need to download a program called a text-editor to create the code for these projects.

Visit www.maxw.com for more info on downloading text editors.

STEP 1: Find the Sublime Text website

www.sublimetext.com

Sublime Text

Open your web browser and visit **www.sublimetext.com**.

STEP 2: Download

Download

Click the **Download** button near the top of the web page.

Choose the version you need.

OSX (10.7 or later)

Windows—also

Windows 64 bit

Wait for the download to be complete.

STEP 3: Install the software

Some web browsers will then ask you to run the installation program. Choose "Run."

Installing ...

If this does not happen, don't panic. The installer file should have been downloaded to your computer. Look in your **downloads** folder for it. Double-click on it to start installing your new text editor. You should get a grey box giving you instructions on what to do next. Follow these instructions to complete the installation.

For help go to: www.maxw.com

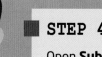

STEP 4: Running Sublime Text

Open **Sublime Text** from your app list.

<HTML>

There are over one-and-a-half billion websites in the world. New sites are added every day, and new phones, tablets, and computers are produced to view them on. For all the different web pages to be read anywhere on any device, there need to be clear standards and codes for how to display them. HTML is the universal language that is used to create all of these web pages.

A program called a web browser is used to view a web page. Commonly used web browsers include Google Chrome, Microsoft Edge, Safari, and Firefox.

HTML pages can contain different components, including images, text, tables, headings, buttons, links, and videos. These components are called elements. Each element has tags and content. The tag explains what type of element to display, and the content tells the browser what to display in that element.

<TAGS>

Tags always start with < and end with > (known as angle brackets).

All elements have an opening tag and most have a closing tag.

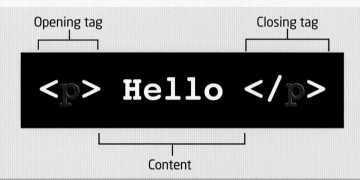

Opening tag   Closing tag

<p> Hello </p>

Content

STEP 5: A simple web page

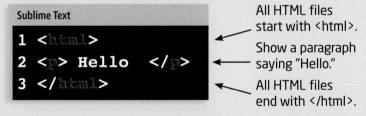

Sublime Text
```
1 <html>
2 <p> Hello </p>
3 </html>
```

All HTML files start with <html>.

Show a paragraph saying "Hello."

All HTML files end with </html>.

STEP 6: Save your page

■ Click **File > Save**.

■ Browse to your documents folder.

■ Type **hello.html** as the file name.

STEP 7: View your page

■ Open your documents folder.

■ Find the **hello.html** file and double-click on it.

■ Your web page should now load in your normal web browser.

Now that you have built a simple web page, we will learn how to add video to the page.

documents/hello.html

Hello

Add Video to a Web Page

Now let's use HTML to add a short video to a web page.

Instead of using paragraphs, we will use the HTML *video* element.

We will also need the *source* element to specify the video's file name.

<source>

This will add a video to the web page.

Sublime Text - gokart.html

<video>

documents/gokart.html

STEP 1: Download a video

Go to **maxw.com/downloads** and click on the **Go kart** video.

maxw.com/downloads
Downloads

You can use your own file if you prefer. Make sure you change "gokart.mp4" in your HTML code

STEP 2: Move it to your documents folder

Find the gokart.mp4 file and drag it to your My Documents folder. (On a Mac drag it to Documents.)

Downloads

gokart.mp4

gokart.mp4

gokart.mp4

My documents

STEP 3: Start a new HTML file

Start your text editor or click **File > New**.

Type symbols like these "">/; very carefully.

STEP 4: Type in the code

Carefully type this into your text editor.

```
1  <!DOCTYPE html>
2  <html>
3  <p>    Watch this  </p>
4  <video width="720" height="480" controls>
5    <source src="gokart.mp4" type="video/mp4">
6  </video>
7  </html>
```

This tells the browser the file contains the latest version of HTML.

All HTML files start with the <html> tag.

Show a paragraph saying "Watch this."

Add a video element to the page. Set width and height, and show the video controls.

Set the file name and file type.

End the video element.

End the HTML file.

STEP 5: Save your page

- Click **File > Save**.
- Go to your documents folder.
- Type **video.html** as the file name.

STEP 6: View your page

Open your documents folder and double-click the **video.html** file.

Click play.

STEP 7: Arrange your screen

As you start to develop more complex HTML pages, you need to be able to see your code and the HTML page at the same time. Many web developers set up their screen so the HTML is on the left side and their web page is shown on the right side.

Resize your text editor and browser windows so your screen looks like this:

```
1  <!DOCTYPE html>
2  <html>
3  <p>      Watch this    </p>
4  <video width="720" height="480" controls>
5    <source src="gokart.mp4" type="video/mp4">
6  </video>
7  </html>
```

After you have made a change to your HTML code in the text editor, save your file.

To see the effects of your changes, you need to reload the web page by clicking the refresh icon.

Don't forget you need to put the mp4 video file in the same folder as your HTML document.

EXPERIMENT

Change the width and height properties from 720 and 480. Remember to save and refresh your page to see the changes.

Try downloading a different video to your documents folder. Change your code to show the new video.

Add another video element with another source element to show two videos on the page.

Slow Motion

Some things happen so quickly, it can be hard to see them: a balloon bursting for example. Other events happen very slowly, so that you don't notice them—such as a flower opening its petals.

Let's add some code to our video player that enables us to change the speed of the video so we don't miss anything in it.

1 The HTML code you type tells a web page which elements to include in a page. To make things happen on a web page when a button is pressed, or when the page loads, we need to use JavaScript. To add JavaScript to a web page, you use a <script> element.

2 **This is how to use the script element.**

```
<script>
```
← This shows the start of some JavaScript.

```
</script>
```
← This shows the end.

3 **We also need to give the video player a name.**

```
<video id="vp">
```

The **id** attribute is how we set the name of an element.

Our id is **vp** (short for video player).

4 **Finally we need some JavaScript to change the speed.**

This selects the video element so we can make changes to it.

This is where we set the speed of the video.

```
document.getElementById('vp').playbackRate=1
```

■ **STEP 1: Download a video**

Go to **maxw.com/downloads** and click on **Burst video**.

maxw.com/downloads
Downloads
Go kart video.
Slide video.
Burst video.

You can use your own file if you prefer. Make sure you change "burst.mp4" in your HTML code too.

■ **STEP 2: Move it to your documents folder**

Find the burst.mp4 file and drag it to your My Documents folder. (On a Mac drag it to Documents.)

burst.mp4
Downloads

burst.mp4

burst.mp4
My documents

STEP 3: Type in the code

Start a new file in your text editor, and type in this code.

```
1    <!DOCTYPE html>
2    <html>
3    <video id="vp" width="640" height="480" controls>
4        <source src="burst.mp4" type="video/mp4">
5    </video>
6    <script>
7        document.getElementById('vp').playbackRate=0.5;
8    </script>
9    </html>
```

Set the document type to HTML.
Start the HTML page.
Show the video element. We call it "vp" by setting its id attribute.
Set the file name and file type.
End the video element.
Start the script.
Set the video player speed to 0.5 (half speed).
End the script.
End the HTML file.

STEP 4: Save your page

■ Click **File > Save**.

■ Go to your documents folder.

■ Type **speed.html** as the file name.

STEP 5: View your page

Open your documents folder and double-click the **speed.html** file.

Click **Play** to see the balloon burst in slow motion!

documents/speed.html

Ultra Slow Motion

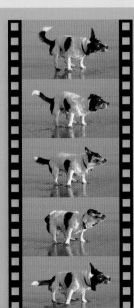

Cameras can film things in slow motion. Normal video cameras take 24–30 fps (frames per second). Slow-motion cameras take hundreds of frames every second. This allows them to capture much more detail than a conventional camera. When the video from a slow-motion camera is played back at 30 fps, it will automatically slow down the action—and add extra detail.

■ EXPERIMENT

Arrange your screen so you can see your code and your web browser—see step 7 on page 19 for help.

Try changing 0.5 in line 7 of your code to a smaller number like 0.2 or 0.1. Save your code and refresh your web page. Play the video. What happens?

Change the playbackRate to a larger number like 2 or 3. What happens when you play the video?

21

Pause and Play

Pausing or stopping a video at the right moment can be fun! Do it just as something is about to happen—like jumping in a swimming pool

Let's add some code to our HTML page to pause a video. We will need to add a button element to do this. Another button and piece of code will allow it to play again.

There are several new bits of code we will need to use in this project.

We will need to add buttons to the page.

```
<button onclick>="playVideo()">Play</button>
```

| Use this tag to start the button element. | An event — the button is clicked. | When the event happens, run this function. | Show this text on the button. | End the button element. |

We also need a script section to run the function.

```
<script>
```
← Start some JavaScript.

```
function
```
← We will write simple functions in JavaScript to play and pause the video.

```
id="vp"
```
← So our script knows which element is playing the video we will give the video player an id, or a name, "**vp**."

STEP 1: Download a video

Go to **maxw.com/downloads** and click on **Slide video**.

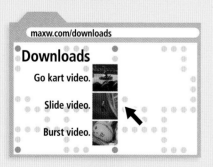

STEP 2: Move it to your documents folder

Find the burst.mp4 file and drag it to your My Documents folder. (On a Mac drag it to Documents.)

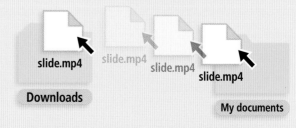

STEP 3: Type in the code

Open your text editor and create a new file. Type in this code.

```
1   <!DOCTYPE html>
2   <html>
3   <video id="vp" width="480" height="720">
4     <source src="slide.mp4" type="video/mp4">
5   </video>
6   <button onclick="playVideo()"Play</button>
7   <button onclick="pauseVideo()"Pause</button>
8   <script>
9   function playVideo(){
10      document.getElementById('vp').play();
11  }
12  function pauseVideo(){
13      document.getElementById('vp').pause();
14  }
15  </script>
16  </html>
```

← Set the document type.

← Start the HTML page.

← Add a video element to the page.

← Set the video file name and file type.

← End the video element.

← Add the play button. It will run the playVideo function when it is clicked.

← Add the pause button. It will run the pauseVideo function when it is clicked.

← Start the script section.

← Define a function called **playVideo**.

← Retrieve the element called "vp" (the video) and make it play.

← End the function.

← Define a function called **pauseVideo**.

← Retrieve the element called "vp" (the video) and make it pause.

← End the function.

← End the script section.

← End the HTML file.

STEP 4: Save your page

■ Click **File > Save**.

■ Go to your documents folder.

■ Type **slide.html** as the file name.

STEP 5: View your page

Open your documents folder and double-click the **slide.html** file.

documents/slide.html

Try clicking the Play and Pause buttons.

Play   Pause

■ EXPERIMENT

Try downloading a different video to your documents folder. Change your code to show the new video.

Change the text on the play and pause buttons.

Insert a <br> element at the start of line 6. Save and refresh your code— what happens?

Streaming

We are all used to watching movies and listening to music on computers, mobile phones, or tablets.

We can pick from thousands of options and start listening or watching immediately. But until recently that was impossible. A technology called streaming has made it possible. But how does streaming work?

Before computers

Music was stored on records, audio tapes, or CDs.

Movies were stored on videotapes or DVDs.

Downloading

Movies and music can be downloaded. This means saving a copy of a large file onto your own computer. Downloading is slow for high quality movies and music and uses up a lot of storage.

Why do movies take up so much memory?

High quality movies take up a lot of memory because each frame of the movie is made of almost a million pixels. There are sometimes 60 frames in each second. If a movie is two hours long that's 1,000,000 pixels x 60 frames x 60 seconds x 120 minutes. That math means you need to download 432,000,000,000 pixels!

Streaming

When you stream music or a movie, it will start playing almost right away. This is because the movie is broken down into millions of tiny parts. Each part is downloaded, then played immediately.

Once it has finished downloading, the next part starts loading automatically. This means you don't need to wait and you don't need lots of memory to store movies. But you do need a good internet connection!

Downloading is kind of like having a bath.

You have to wait until the bath is filled up before getting in!

Streaming is more like having a shower!

You can get in right away!

Embedding Video

Some streaming sites allow you to put their videos on to your own web page.

Instead of downloading the video, it is streamed from the original website. To make a video play on your own website, you need to use some code to embed it—to put it on your page.

STEP 1: Get the embed code

Choose a video from YouTube or another similar website.

Click the **Share** button. Look below the video.

Click the **Embed** button.

Right-click on the embed code.

Click **Copy**.

STEP 2: A new file

Start your text editor, or click **File > New**.

STEP 3: Type in the code

Enter the code below. Line 3 is where your embedded code goes.

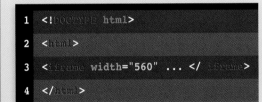

```
1  <!DOCTYPE html>
2  <html>
3  <iframe width="560" ... </iframe>
4  </html>
```

← Set the document type.
← Start the HTML page.
← Embed your video.
← End the HTML.

> **Right-click your mouse, then click paste to add the embed code here.**

> **Try playing the video.**

STEP 4: Save your page

- Click **File > Save**.
- Go to your documents folder.
- Type **videos.html** as the file name.

STEP 5: View your page

Open your documents folder and double-click the **videos.html** file.

EXPERIMENT

Try adding more embedded videos to your page. Copy another embed code, then click at the start of line 4. Paste in your new code.

Why won't some videos play?

Most YouTube videos will play if you embed them in your HTML page. But some won't. This is because some videos have extra security settings—this means they can only be played online in a full website. Try embedding different sorts of videos: TV clips, cartoons, or help videos.

Camera Code

documents/camera.html

In this project, we will access the camera in your computer. By using HTML and JavaScript code, we will display the camera or webcam on your screen.

We will use the video element again in this code. But instead of setting the source to be a downloaded video, we will connect it to a stream of data from the camera.

Split into two sections

In this project we don't have anything to put in the head section, but we will use the body tag.

To keep things organized, more complex HTML pages are split into two sections.

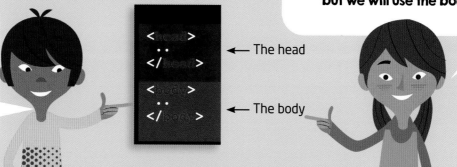

← The head

← The body

We have used many of the elements in HTML several times. Tags like <html> and <video> will have become familiar and should make sense to you. The <body> tag is simple to use too.

However, sometimes coders use sections of code that are much more advanced. In this project, there are two very complex lines of code. We will look at what they do, but you don't need to understand them in the same detail as the basic tags.

```
navigator.mediaDevices.getUserMedia({video:true})
```

This will get a stream of data from one of the media (audio or video) input devices connected to you computer.

This limits the media to video only.

```
.then(function(stream){video.srcObject=stream;});
```

If a video media device is found, then run this code.

Use the stream of video data.

This connects the video element, and sets its source to be the new video stream.

Using the camera in HTML and JavaScript can be quite tricky and depends on how your camera is set up. Updates to web browsers can affect how things work. Check **maxw.com** for help and more info.

STEP 1: Start a new HTML file

Open your text editor, or click **File** > **New**.

STEP 2: Start a new HTML file

Carefully type in the following code.

```
1   <!DOCTYPE html>                                          ← Set the document type.
2   <html>                                                   ← Start the HTML page.
3   <body>                                                   ← Start the body section of the page.
4     <video id="vp" autoplay="true"></video>               ← Add the video element.
5   </body>                                                  ← End the body section.
6   <script>                                                 ← Start the script section.
7     var video document.getElementById('vp');               ← Store the video element in
                                                                a variable called "video."
8     navigator.mediaDevices.getUserMedia({video:true})      ← Get the webcam from the devices
                                                                connected to the computer.
9     .then(function(stream){video.srcObject stream;});      ← Connect the stream of video from
                                                                the camera to the video element.
10  </script>                                                ← End the script section.
11  </html>                                                  ← End the html file.
```

STEP 3: Save your page

- Click **File** > **Save**.
- Go to your documents folder.
- Type **camera.html** as the file name.

STEP 4: View your page

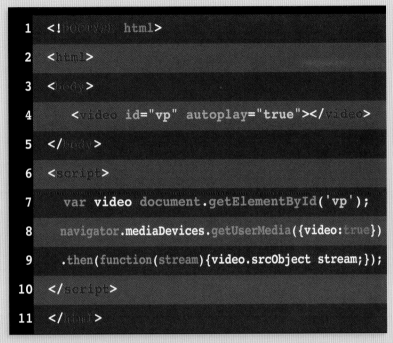

documents/camera.html

Open your documents folder and double-click the **camera.html** file.

Your browser will ask to use your camera. Click "Allow."

But if other websites ask to use your camera, always check with an adult first.

■ EXPERIMENT

Try adding width and height attributes to your video element code in line 4. Save and refresh your code.

On page 17, you added a paragraph of text to your HTML. Add a <p> tag inside your <body> section.

Look back to page 23 to see how to add the controls to your video player. What happens if you press pause?

Change video:true to audio:true. Turn your volume down a little before you save and refresh.

Camera with Filters

It is much simpler to use the Webcam in Scratch. By making the webcam image transparent (see-through) we can also add some extra effects.

Let's color in the Scratch screen's background, which will show through the partly transparent camera image. Code will then allow the background to change color—what do you think will happen?

STEP 1: Start Scratch

scratch.mit.edu

Start Scratch and click **Create**.

STEP 2: Video extension

Add the Video Sensing extension.

Click **Add Extension**. Click **Video sensing**.

Video sensing

STEP 3: No cats

Sprite1

Click the blue x to delete the cat sprite.

How do webcams work?

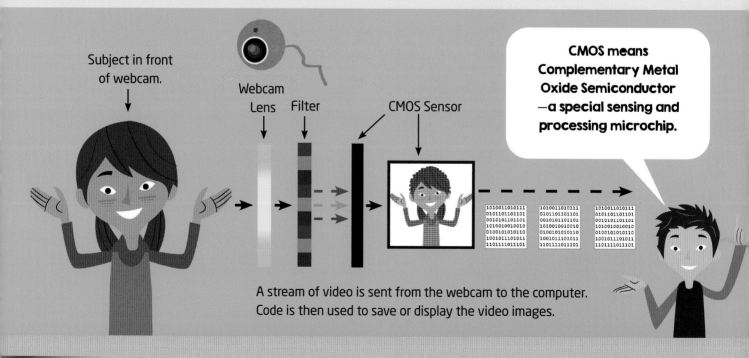

Subject in front of webcam.

Webcam Lens Filter

CMOS Sensor

CMOS means Complementary Metal Oxide Semiconductor —a special sensing and processing microchip.

A stream of video is sent from the webcam to the computer. Code is then used to save or display the video images.

STEP 4: The background

Click the
Backdrops tab.

Click the
Convert to Bitmap button.

Click the
Fill button.

Choose red.

Fill the backdrop in red.

STEP 5: Turn on the camera

Drag these blocks into the **Scripts** area.

when 🚩 clicked ← Run this code when the green flag is pressed.

turn video on ▼ ← Turn the video camera on.

set video transparency to 50 ← Make the video image 50% transparent.

clear graphic effects ← Remove any color effects (we'll add more later!).

🏳️ Click the green flag to test your code.

A video of you should appear in the stage area of Scratch. You should look slightly red!

STEP 6: Add some effects

Drag these blocks into the **Scripts** area.

when up arrow ▼ key pressed
When the **up arrow key** is pressed, run this code.

change colour ▼ effect by 5
Change the background color by a small amount.

when down arrow ▼ key pressed
← When the **down arrow key** is pressed, run this code.

change colour ▼ effect by -5
Change the background color by a small amount. By using -5, this has the opposite effect of the up arrow.

🏳️ Click the green flag again.

Try pressing the up and down arrow.

EXPERIMENT

In step 6, change 5 and -5 to -1 and 1. What happens?

Experiment with different backgrounds—try patterns or shapes.

The color of the video should change!

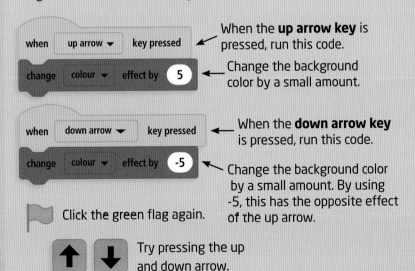

The Scratch Screen

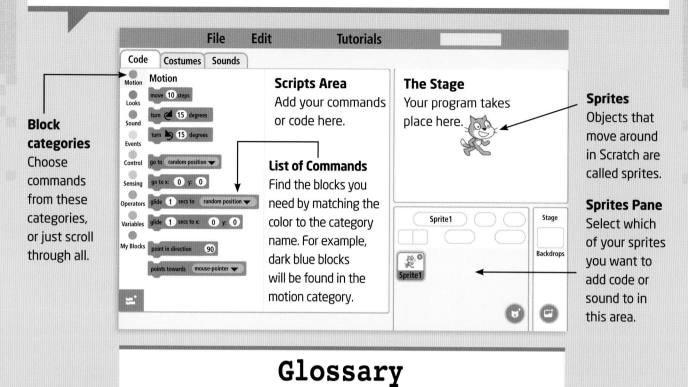

File   Edit   Tutorials

Code   Costumes   Sounds

Motion

Motion
Looks
Sound
Events
Control
Sensing
Operators
Variables
My Blocks

move 10 steps
turn 15 degrees
turn 15 degrees
go to random position
go to x: 0 y: 0
glide 1 secs to random position
glide 1 secs to x: 0 y: 0
point in direction 90
points towards mouse-pointer

Block categories
Choose commands from these categories, or just scroll through all.

Scripts Area
Add your commands or code here.

List of Commands
Find the blocks you need by matching the color to the category name. For example, dark blue blocks will be found in the motion category.

The Stage
Your program takes place here.

Sprite1

Sprite1

Stage

Backdrops

Sprites
Objects that move around in Scratch are called sprites.

Sprites Pane
Select which of your sprites you want to add code or sound to in this area.

Glossary

amplifier
An electrical device that makes sounds louder

analog (sound)
A real sound wave that keeps changing all the time

attribute
Extra information about an HTML element, such as the address of a video

bug
An error in a program that stops it from working properly

code block
A draggable instruction icon used in Scratch

debug
Removing bugs (or errors) from a program

digital (sound)
A sound wave that has been stored as a series of numbers, changing thousands of times per second

element
One of the objects making up a web page, such as a paragraph or image

embedding
Placing an element on a web page, but getting its content from a different website

event
Something that has happened while a program is running, such as a component being clicked or touched

function
A reusable section of code combining a number of commands

HTML (HyperText Markup Language)
The language used to build web pages

loop
Repeating one or more commands a number of times

octave
The distance between two musical notes that are eight notes apart

pixel
A tiny dot on a computer screen, combined in the thousands to display pictures

refresh
To load a web page again in the web browser so changes to the page can be seen

right-click
Clicking the right mouse button on a sprite or icon

semitone
Half a tone on a musical scale, such as the interval between C and C#

software
A computer program containing instructions written in code

sprite
An object with a picture on it that moves around the stage

synthesize (sound)
To create an artificial sound using a computer (not a recording)

Bugs & Debugging

When you find your code isn't working as expected, stop and look through each command you have put in. Think about what you want it to do and what it is really telling the computer to do. If you are entering one of the programs in this book, check you have not missed a line. Some things to check:

▮ SCRATCH

Select sprites before adding code:

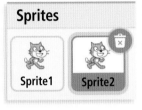

Before you add code to a sprite, click on it in the **Sprites pane**. This will select it and make sure the code is assigned to it.

Right color, wrong code?

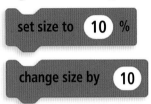

Be precise. Many code blocks look very similar but do completely different things.

▮ HTML

If your HTML code doesn't seem to be working properly, save your code, then refresh your browser. Look for clues about where the problem might be.

Look for patterns
The end of line 3 looks different.

Highlighted code
Unexpected code may be highlighted.

Text color
This div tag is a different color.

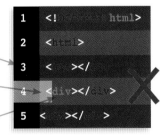

Be careful with symbols like ">/ and ;. If any are missing or in the wrong place, your code won't work.

If your code has a **<script>** section, you can also try looking for errors in the browser.

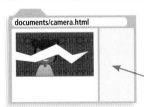

In your browser, click the **View** menu, choose **Developer** then **Developer Tools**.

The developer tools show up here.

The error message may be confusing.

But it will tell you where the error is. In this case, it's in line 7.

---

tags
Special words in an HTML document surrounded by angle brackets < > defining an element

stage
The place in Scratch that sprites move around on

variable
A value used to store information in a program that can change

web browser
Program used to view web pages such as Google Chrome or Mircosoft Edge

Index

Further information

Coding for Kids
by Camille McCue (For Dummies, 2019)

Coding Projects in Scratch
by Jon Woodcock (DK Children, 2019)

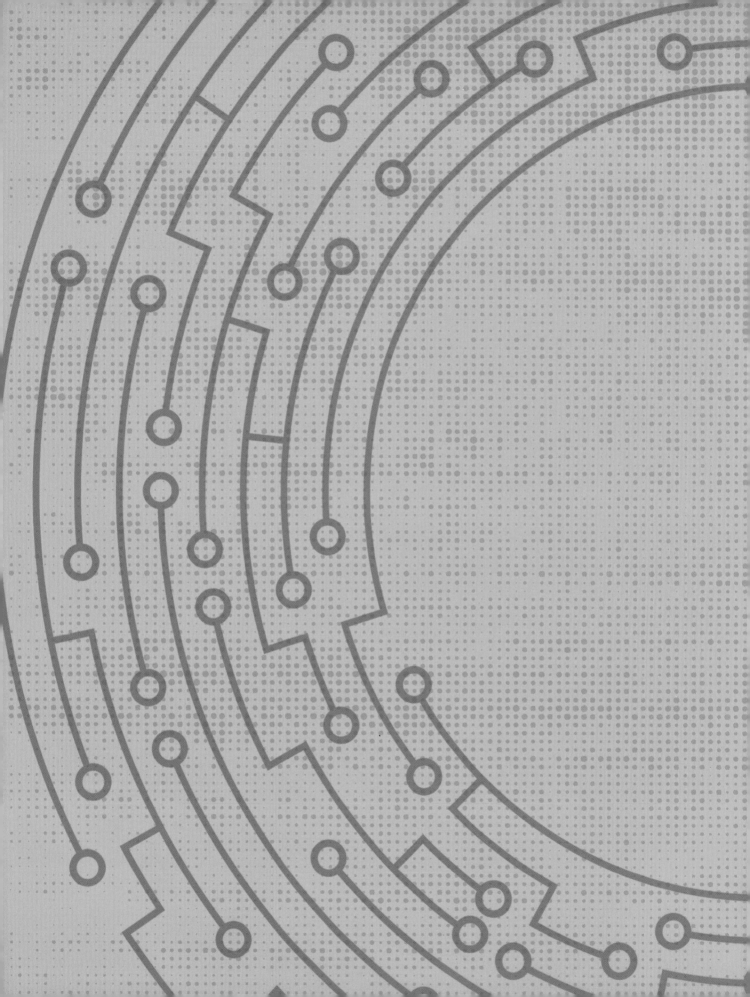